MY FIRST ART BOOK OF BABY ANIMALS

Coloring Book 2 Year Olds

EDUCANDO KIDS

Let's Color the Baby Animals!

Have fun!

cub

calf

calf

cub

calf

cub

hatchling

colt

infant

duckling

chick

Puppy

Piglet

kit

foal

lamb

calf

This is a Bleed Through Page If You Are Using a Coloring Marker or Pen!
Find Other Great Titles By searching for Educando Kids on Your Favorite Book Retailer
Amazon.Com | Barnes & Noble (BN.Com) | Books A Million (BAM.Com)

EDUCANDO
KIDS

kit

pinkie

Printed in the USA
CPSIA information can be obtained
at www.ICGtesting.com
LVHW072208211123
764606LV00049B/1734